Icebreakers tha Engaged Teams and Set the Tone for Your Audience

Leaders and Presenters, Own the Room and Create a Team of Promoters

Written By: C. R. Chestian

been executed to present accurate, up to date, and reliable, complete information. No warranties of any kind are declared or implied. Readers acknowledge that the author is not engaging in the rendering of legal, financial, medical or professional advice. The content within this book has been derived from various sources. Please consult a licensed professional before attempting any techniques outlined in this book.

By reading this document, the reader agrees that under no circumstances is the author responsible for any losses, direct or indirect, which are incurred as a result of the use of the information contained within this document, including, but not limited to, — errors, omissions, or inaccuracies.

Table of Contents

Introduction

Chapter 1 - Icebreaker Purpose

Chapter 2 - Icebreakers for Engaged Teams

Chapter 3 - Icebreakers for the Team of Promoters

Chapter 4 - Icebreakers that Set the Tone

Chapter 5 - Icebreakers that Own the Room

Conclusion

Introduction

We are in a world where grabbing attention is a challenge. Understanding the additional work you have to do to get people engaged with your message has become the roadblock to employees getting promoted and leaders getting stuck in their current positions. Are you having little success convincing the decision-maker at your presentation to buy into your pitch? Numbers don't lie, but they no longer own the room the way they used to. Your message or pitch has to dance, sing and shout. Powerpoint or the "deck" can no longer be the main selling point for the conversation, but it's still needed to guide the conversation.

How do we grab attention, engage our employees and make the sale? We break the ice! Not just a few easy jokes either, but icebreakers that stand the test of time and promote your message into a memorable experience. You could pass down this book to your leaders as you ascend the corporate ladder or to the rookie prepping for their first presentation as you enjoy the corner office. Stop wasting time on google, spending hours searching for the right icebreaker when you can have everything you need in this handy guide created for your success. Having all you need in one place can help reduce the stress when preparing for the big day. Whether it's a weekly or monthly meeting, you can plan out your content for the entire quarter using the icebreakers in this book. Depending on your audience for your next sales pitch, you might find a favorite that genuinely resonates with the product you are pitching.

Setting the tone and owning the room is the first step to ensure your message is memorable. Using a good video can be great, but the video isn't about you, the messenger! Conditioning your audience's minds to hang on your every word is accomplished through the icebreaker exercise. Don't just warm up the crowd, but create an environment of your own your audience yearns to be a part of with you. Whether you have a group, you have been working with for years or are a newcomer. You will make a massive impression on your audience once you implement these icebreakers at the beginning of each meeting.

Chapter 1

Icebreaker Purpose

An icebreaker is an exercise where people facilitate the activity or question. The icebreaker helps members of a group begin forming themselves into a team. Icebreakers are often used as a game to "warm-up" the group by assisting them in getting to know each other.

This generalization is excellent, but what more can you gain with them? Take a step back and ask yourself, did the icebreaker accomplish people getting to know one another? Would the information gathered by your audience about each other at some point be shared organically? We often use icebreakers to get the ball rolling, such as first names, history at the company, or a quick joke to get everyone laughing. You will find that many of the ice breakers used today don't give you a big bang for your buck as some of the information shared would be revealed over time organically through a natural conversation. As I stated before, jokes are easy but asking an icebreaker to share a funny story hits two birds with one stone, and the best part is you not asking for a funny story!

Icebreaker questions can take your team and audience to a whole new level if used appropriately. Create vulnerability, strengthening the bond and trust people will have for you. The icebreakers shared in this book will take your audience into a state of focus after capturing their attention entirely with the questions you have asked. Most people expect icebreakers to be funny, and I offer ones that will lead some folks rolling on the floor from laughter. However, the goal here is to grab the attention so deep that there can be no distraction from your message as you deliver it. Icebreakers that can cater to your topic and takeaways help create a memorable experience. Have your audience thinking about it the very next day when you hit it out of the park with icebreakers.

You will read in the following chapters how I have broken out these questions based on the desired outcome. To create an engaged team, you build collectively and in small units simultaneously. By breaking out and coming in, your team or audience helps with the heavy lifting, as smaller groups can get more accomplished when four or fewer people are talking. Building an accountability partner structure helps create promoters within your organization. For the leader, an important note for your accountability structure is to include your employees on how often they want to rotate partners. Supporting a rotation keeps the exercises reusable and builds engagement as different personalities interact.

When presenting, try not to go over the amount of four people when setting up the accountability structure. You want to ensure everyone has enough time to speak to the icebreaker. If you have minimal time, stick with just two partners in the accountability structure so you can get the biggest bang for your buck.

This structure allows you to begin to read the room. How did people react? Who may need convincing of your message? At this stage, you have already started your purpose for the meeting. You can now play out your plan of attack with your messaging. The time you have allotted, which should be no more than fifteen minutes, your accountability partners should be coming back excited and engaged, primed, ready for your message! Jokes will be a method when selecting an icebreaker at some point when it will benefit the outcome the most. This step is how you create promoters.

Chapter 2

Icebreakers for Engaged Teams

The following icebreakers you would share in a group setting with everyone participating. The desired outcome is to promote curiosity about everyone in attendance so that the conversation can continue even after the meeting is over. The answers should be relatively short, providing your group of participants enough time to answer. It is also an excellent way to learn a few essential items critical to your audience.

Set the expectation before the icebreaker that their answer will more than likely be short due to the icebreaker asked. You will notice we could add a "why?" to any of the questions. However, it is the reason curiosity will ensue after the meeting is over. I just wanted to note the added benefit of the questions if you see fit to reuse them in the future, provided you have more time for lengthy answers but let the organic connections occur. You will find out later on from your audience anything you may facilitate digging deeper into after the feedback guides your next move. Always consider the topic of your discussion and which icebreaker correlates best.

- *If you could take 3 things to a desert island what would they be?*
- *What is the reason you get up in the morning?*
- *Would you rather have invisibility or flight?*

- *Describe your weekend in one word?*
- *Which do you prefer more, dogs or cats?*
- *What would your entrance theme song be?*
- *If you were a potato or (sweet), what way would you like to be cooked?*
- *What animal would you choose to be?*
- *What song describes your life right now?*
- *Would you rather win an Olympic medal or a Nobel prize?*
- *If you had to describe how you're feeling right now as a weather pattern, what's your forecast?*
- *Describe your communication style in 3 words?*
- *If you were setting off to Jupiter and could take only one luxury item with you, what would it be?*
- *It's karaoke night, what song are you submitting to sing?*

- *What season would you be?*
- *Which fruit or vegetable would you want to be?*
- *Where would you live if you could pick any country?*
- *If you could instantly speak any language, which one would you choose?*
- *Physically what age do you wish you could be stuck in forever?*
- *Do you want to be the funniest or smartest person in the room?*
- *Your next vacation would you visit a volcano or a rainforest?*
- *You can change your first name to any other name. What is your new name?*
- *Morning person or a night owl, which are you?*

Chapter 3

Icebreakers for the Team of Promoters

Creating a team of promoters is where you will implement the accountability partner structure. Partnering your folks together allows them to go in-depth with the icebreakers and helps to form bonds that might have otherwise not formed. This meeting should be an exercise where you set the stage and give them no more than fifteen minutes to work through the icebreakers provided. You can provide three to five; however, most times, they will only hit three within the allotted time. Once time is up, the partners share each other's responses. There is a lot to gain from how well people enjoyed the experience with what information they retained from the accountability partner icebreaker session. Do not disclose that they will share each other's responses, as this will help keep your audience on its toes with the momentum in your favor. This process will help you learn a great deal regarding your audience and how they react to one another. You assign the partners for your team. If you are presenting, have your audience partner with the person in front of them. If it's a small group, have them partner with the person opposite of them. We do this as most people will select someone they are already vulnerable or connected to through friendship. By keeping the partners as random and unknown, you will have genuine feedback on the experience. Here you will apply the accountability partner structure. It is here we will begin to include the why to the icebreaker.

- *What's your favorite joke to tell? Why do you find it funny?*
- *What's the strangest gift you've ever received? Who gave it to you?*
- *What's your biggest guilty pleasure? Why?*
- *What song or tune always gets stuck in your head? If you know the words, can you sing it?*
- *When having fun, what's the scariest thing you've ever done? Where was it?*
- *What's your first thought in the morning after you wake up? Last thought at night?*
- *What do you think the company mascot should be? Why?*
- *What's something you're looking forward to, and why?*

- *What's something you're worried about most? Why?*
- *What is one goal you desire to accomplish in your current role at the company? Have you started?*
- *What would be your superpower if you could have one today, and what would you do with it? How would you benefit?*
- *What one question would you wish to know the truth? Why?*
- *If you could live in any sitcom, which one would it be? Can you sing the theme song?*
- *You have 36 hours in a day. How would you spend the extra 12 hours? How would you benefit?*
- *Instantly you pick up a new skill. What would that new skill be? How would you benefit?*
- *When you're feeling stressed, how do you deal with it? Why those methods?*

- *What life-changing advice have you received? Who gave it to you?*
- *What's something people don't know about you? Do you typically not share it?*
- *You must wear a T-shirt with one word on it for a year. Which word do you choose? What color is the T-shirt?*
- *What's the most useful item you've purchased this year? Why did you buy it?*
- *You're cooking for the whole team; what is your signature dish? What would you make for dessert?*
- *What's one thing you wish could be automated in your job? Have you explored if it's possible?*
- *Why did you apply to work for this company? What were your other options at the time?*

- *Name one thing you would change if you ran the world? Would you run it with anyone or solo?*

- *Where were you born, and did you grow up there? Did your family grow up there too?*

- *As a child, which food did you hate? Have you come to love it, or still hate it?*

- *What's your favorite tradition or holiday? Explain?*

- *You receive a time machine. Would you go back in time or into the future? What would you hope to see?*

- *What is one thing that keeps you here at this company? Why is that one thing necessary to you?*

- *You decide to remove one thing from your daily routine, what would it be? Why?*

- *Are you a traveler or a homebody? Why?*

- *Is there anything you have completed anything on your "bucket list"? Last item you completed?*
- *What's the weirdest food you've ever eaten? Where were you when you ate it?*
- *You have a personal assistant that follows you around constantly. What do you have them do? How much would you pay them?*

Chapter 4

Icebreakers that Set the Tone

You always want your team or audience engaged. Setting the tone for your message is essential. What's the takeaway or the call-to-action for your audience? Coordinating that with a solid icebreaker can be the difference between creating a memorable message or just some blocked-out time on someone's calendar. If you inform your audience of something new, using humor is the best way to get started as it will prepare their minds for the latest information. Suppose the message is more of a call-to-action. In that case, an icebreaker that can resonate with a passion and further promote their ambition can help create an actionable outcome for your audience. The difference between your audience learning or taking action is how you prepare them to receive you. Learning is an action on its own, but anyone can learn something. Learning is not the same as retaining information. The icebreaker should prep the mind for the value you are about to deliver so that they hang onto your every word. Your preparation for your call-to-action should have them ready to race out of their seats once you have finished. A call-to-action might involve an icebreaker at the beginning and end of your message to ensure it hits home for your audience. The following icebreakers are broken into Learning and Call-to-Action to assist with selecting your desired outcome.

Learning:

- Start with a joke, preferably your favorite. The one that makes you laugh the most, but make sure it's suitable for your audience. If no one laughs, say you should have known when your mom found it funny.

- If you don't have a favorite joke visit laughfactory.com, and you will find something relevant on the first page to use as your opener. Make sure you practice with someone, and you will have an engaged audience hanging on every word.

- Share a funny story about you and take that first step of creating vulnerability.

- If you already know it's a tough crowd, involve them from the beginning and ask them their names and opinions about what you are wearing. Do they like your dress, your tie, maybe your T-shirt! Ask about three people. Please talk about your thought process and be extreme about the ideas you have had when going into the meeting and how they impacted your clothing choice. You will have to be quick on your feet. After you have had three audience members respond, you should be able to layout a quick agreement and apology to get the crowd going with laughter, as not everyone will agree. However, everyone will enjoy your playfulness. An example:

- You: Morning, Sir! And your name?
- Audience Member: Josh
- You: Ok, Josh, how do you like the outfit? Are you buying the same today, or should I burn the shirt after leaving the meeting?

- Audience Member: Shoes are nice, but the tie could have been darker.
- You: There you have it, folks, blinding the man before we get started. At least I can keep the shirt!

Call-to-Action

- It is an inspiring, brief story about what the day's topic or focus means to you.
- A fun anecdote about the last time you had this group of people together or the last time you led a similar meeting with your call-to-action as the outcome.
- It is a story about your first encounter with the group, product, or idea you'll be discussing at that event.
- When did you last feel limitless optimism?

- What's a time when someone did something you appreciated (at work or in another context), but you didn't let them know? What held you back?
- When you pass from this earth, what do you want the memory of you to be?
- A typical story like a fairy tale can represent your call to action.
  - The grasshopper and the ant
  - The tortoise and the hare
  - Jack and the beanstalk
  - Little red riding hood
  - Cinderella

Chapter 5

Icebreakers that Own the Room

This last section is more about owning the room than icebreakers. At this point, you should have an audience, whether it's a meeting or presentation, hanging onto every word you say. A good meeting or presentation always allows the audience to interact with the information provided through a Q&A segment. There may be someone in the audience who does not want to wait for the Q&A. Maybe the segment as a whole starts to shift after one question is asked by your audience, and you may have to go on the side of diffusion to bring your audience back—some tips for doing it effortlessly and gain even more confidence and trust from your audience.

First, welcome the challenge from the audience! A disagreement with you is a potential passion in your group. Leverage that energy to bring your room into your message's benefits. Never argue an opinion, as everyone is entitled to their thoughts. Agree with their concerns and rely on your facts. Understand them and walk through their challenge with them and the crowd. If you did your homework, you should already know what opposition would be present. Express your understanding of their concerns and address them. If you do not have the answer ready at the moment, be open to taking it offline and highlight that it's a point you look forward to reviewing with them. Do not take the disagreement personally, as you shouldn't carry expectations to win over 100% of the audience. There is always the one who doesn't want to be engaged. It happens in every industry and every conversation. Think of the last toothpaste commercial you saw. It's almost always nine out of ten dentists that agree, but you don't see anyone looking for the one dentist that disagrees. You can also include your audience to see if anyone shares the same concern. Quickly gauge if this is an outlier or maybe you missed an essential item while delivering your message. Mistakes happen, you may be nervous, but you can own the room by owning and covering your content.

Second, if you are going into a conversation and already know the most significant obstacle impacting your audience from receiving your message, address it. Whether it is something about you or who you are representing, talk about it and show you have no fear and own the obstacle. If you are selling something and it impedes the transition, address it. Everything you can get out into the open will prepare your audience's minds for hanging onto your every word. After you have completed your first icebreaker, lead into owning the obstacle. Not only did you take the first step of vulnerability, but you also will gain respect from taking ownership of their concerns without avoiding them.

Third and last, find what resonates for them in the message. The majority of your audience will have a commonplace shared and be committed to your messaging. You will know this by reading the room as you deliver your message. With the time you have allotted, and how your content hits home with your audience, you can pause to check in with your group for questions. After you have completed delivering your message, you should always end with key take-aways or your call-to-action. Remember to share your story, tie in your opening joke or remind them of the icebreaker exercise. You create value in those experiences based on your selected method to start preparing their minds for your words. Ultimately owning the room is embracing the challenge of tough questions and disagreements, owning the obstacle before delivering the message, and driving home the purpose you asked people to take time out of their day for to experience.

Leave a Review if you enjoyed this Icebreaker Guide!

Conclusion

Bring value to every meeting or presentation you have. Make it an experience, not just a list to be complete where you check the box. Putting the time and effort into creating promoters, engaged teams, and owning the room isn't easy. It can be time-consuming as you prepare your content, search for the best for this or that. Let this book put some time back on your clock so that you don't have to chase the internet for icebreakers. Highlight and take notes and plan out a quarter at a time. You would be amazed how much more you can build upon when you have a three-month head start! Your energy will begin to magnify as you prepare for your content, knowing your audience's takeaways will be impactful.

Divide and conquer your teams and the room. Remember, you don't have to do all the heavy lifting yourself. Create an atmosphere of vulnerability where your audience shares and then takes ownership of reporting their experience to you. The accountability partner structure is a great way to get instant gratification for the work you have already put in. The feedback will help validate your decisions as you continue throughout the meeting. This immediate gain of information will assist you during your Q&A if any opposition arises.

Own the room, deliver the message and build your success through your connection to the audience!

Printed in Great Britain
by Amazon

17540822R00031